The Capture of New Orleans
Union Fleet Takes Control of the Lower Mississippi River

Wendy Vierow

The Rosen Publishing Group's
PowerKids Press™
New York

To my mother

Published in 2004 by The Rosen Publishing Group, Inc.
29 East 21st Street, New York, NY 10010

First Edition

Editor: Frances E. Ruffin

Book Design: Michael de Guzman

Photo Credits: Cover (rifle) photo by Peter Latner, Minnesota Historical Society, (hats) Cindy Reiman; cover (inset), p. 5 © Hulton/Archive/Getty Images; pp. 6, 9, 16, 17, 19, 21 Library of Congress, Prints and Photographs Division; p. 11 Print Collection, Miriam and Ira D. Wallach Division of Art, Prints and Photographs, The New York Public Library, Astor, Lenox and Tilden Foundations; pp. 13, 15 © North Wind Picture Archives; p. 14 Still Picture Branch, National Archives and Records Administration.

Vierow, Wendy.
The capture of New Orleans : Union fleet takes control of the lower Mississippi River / Wendy Vierow.
    p. cm. — (Headlines from history)
Summary: Describes the Union victory at New Orleans during the Civil War.
Includes bibliographical references and index.
  ISBN 0-8239-6222-9 (lib. bdg.)
1. New Orleans (La.)—History—Civil War, 1861–1865—Juvenile literature. [1. New Orleans (La.)—History—Civil War, 1861–1865. 2. United States—History—Civil War, 1861–1865—Campaigns.] I. Title. II. Series.
  F379.N557 V53 2003
  973.7'31—dc21

                                                                              2002000127

Manufactured in the United States of America

CONTENTS

The United States Fights a Civil War

In the spring of 1861, Southern soldiers fired shots at U.S. troops at Fort Sumter, South Carolina. These shots started the **Civil War**, a war between the Northern states and the Southern states, which ended in 1865. There were many reasons for the Civil War, but the most important reason was a disagreement on the issue of **slavery**. Most people in the Northern states thought that slavery was wrong, while most people in the Southern states thought that slavery should be allowed. Many Southerners argued that without the free work of slaves, they would not be able to run their large plantations, or farms.

Worry over the sadness and loss of life caused by the Civil War is shown in this hand-colored photograph of President Abraham Lincoln.

People in the South decided to form their own country. They called their country the **Confederate States of America**, or the Confederacy. They elected Jefferson Davis as president of the 11 Confederate states.

Abraham Lincoln was president of the United States. There were 23 **Union** states when the Civil War began.

The Union and Confederate Navies

When the Civil War broke out, the Union had something that the Confederacy did not. It had an army and a navy. The Union needed to make its navy bigger. Workers turned all kinds of ships, from tugboats to ocean steamers, into ships that could be used to fight.

The Confederacy needed to create a navy. **Confederates** took over ports in the South. However, before leaving Southern ports, the Union navy destroyed many of its own ships. Union officers didn't want Confederates to use Union ships. One sunken Union ship that Confederates raised and repaired was the *Merrimack*. Confederate workers put iron plates on the wooden ship and renamed it the *Virginia*. The iron plates would protect the *Virginia* from cannon fire, making it more difficult to sink.

Union leaders knew the *Virginia* could destroy the Union's wooden ships, so a Union engineer created an iron ship called the *Monitor*. The invention of metal ships ended the age of wooden ships.

This painting shows the battle between the Monitor *and the* Merrimack *(renamed the* Virginia*) near Norfolk, Virginia, in 1862.*

President Lincoln Calls for a Blockade

Within a week after the Confederacy took over Fort Sumter, President Lincoln declared a **blockade** of the Confederacy's coastline. Soon Union ships were stopping Confederate ships from carrying goods to Europe and its colonies in the **West Indies**. Union ships also stopped the Confederacy from receiving goods from other countries and their colonies.

Europeans were unable to receive Southern goods, such as cotton and rice, that were popular overseas. Anyone who could ship these goods overseas could become rich.

Confederate blockade-runners tried to sneak their ships past

Sometimes Union boats were blockade-runners. In 1863, Admiral David Porter attempted to run his boats past a Confederate blockade on the Mississippi River.

Union ships. They used false flags and changed the names on their ships to fool Union sailors. Blockade-runners brought weapons, medicines, and other items from Europe and its colonies to the Confederacy. These supplies helped the Confederacy stay in the fight against the Union.

David G. Farragut Joins the Union Navy

David G. Farragut lived in the South when the Civil War started. Both he and his wife were Southerners. However, they moved to the North shortly after the war began. Farragut joined the Union navy to fight against the South. Farragut had plenty of experience at sea. He was only a boy when he joined the U.S. Navy. He fought the British during the **War of 1812**. By age 12, he was in charge of a captured British ship. In his sixties, Farragut was in excellent shape. Every year on his birthday, he did a handspring.

The Union navy gave Farragut orders to sail up the Mississippi River and capture New Orleans for the Union. New Orleans was the largest city in the South. It was also an important port for the Confederacy.

Farragut looked forward to capturing New Orleans. He wanted to show that he was loyal to the Union, even though he was originally from the South.

When fellow Southerners tried to convince Farragut to remain loyal to the South, he warned Southerners that they would be sorry before they got "through with this business."

A Union Fleet
Sails to New Orleans

New Orleans was guarded by Fort Jackson and Fort St. Philip on the Mississippi River. Both forts had been taken over by the Confederates. To get to New Orleans, Farragut would have to fight at these forts. Farragut was in charge of a large **fleet** of ships. His **foster** brother, David Porter, was in charge of 20 mortar boats. Mortar boats carried mortars, which are short cannons.

On April 18, 1862, the mortar boats fired on the forts. After six days of firing, Farragut decided it was time to act quickly.

This is a painting of Farragut's fleet blasting past Fort Jackson and Fort St. Philip before dawn on April 24, 1862. This action enabled Union ships to steam up the Mississippi River. They were met by Confederate ships that forced the Union ships to stop and fight.

When it became dark, he sailed his fleet by the forts. The Confederates fired on them. They also set Union ships on fire. Farragut's own ship caught on fire. His crew worked hard to put out the fire. Farragut and the Union fleet sailed past both forts. Only four of his ships did not make it through.

The Union Captures New Orleans

Farragut's Union ships sailed toward New Orleans. A small Confederate fleet met them, ready to fight. Farragut and his crew defeated the Confederate fleet. Then Farragut demanded that the city of New Orleans **surrender**. Citizens in New Orleans panicked. They destroyed cotton and other crops, supplies, and ships. They did not want the Union to take anything.

David Farragut became a hero of the North and America's first admiral.

This print shows Confederate brigadier general Johnson K. Duncan boarding the Harriet Lane to surrender Forts Jackson and St. Philip to the Union.

Although Union troops raised the U.S. flag in New Orleans on April 26, 1862, the people of New Orleans would not surrender. Farragut grew tired of waiting. On April 29, 1862, Farragut claimed the city for the Union. Two days later, Union major general Benjamin F. Butler and his troops arrived to take control of the city.

Farragut became a Union hero for capturing New Orleans. After the Civil War ended, Farragut became the first **admiral** in the U.S. Navy.

15

Union Troops Take Control of New Orleans

President Lincoln appointed Major General Butler **governor** of New Orleans. The citizens of New Orleans did not like Butler. Butler took the property of anyone who would not promise to be true to the Union.

Most people in New Orleans would not show respect to the Union. When Butler found out that a man had torn down the U.S. flag that had been raised by Union troops, he had the man arrested, put on trial, and hanged. After

Major General Benjamin F. Butler was a much-disliked Civil War leader.

After the capture of New Orleans, the people in that city were left without food. This print shows Union soldiers handing out food to people in New Orleans.

the hanging, the citizens of New Orleans were more careful about showing their dislike toward the Union.

Many women in New Orleans insulted Union troops, however. Butler threatened to arrest any woman who insulted a Union soldier. Almost all the insults stopped, but the people of New Orleans still disliked Butler.

African Americans Join the Union Army

After Butler arrived in New Orleans, he called upon free African Americans to join the Union army. This angered citizens of New Orleans and many Southerners.

Although the Union navy accepted African Americans, the Union army would not permit them to join. In July 1862, Congress passed laws to let African Americans join the Union army. Then on September 22, 1862, President Lincoln issued the **Emancipation Proclamation**.

The Emancipation Proclamation stated that slaves in Confederate states "shall be then, thenceforth, and forever free,"

When Abraham Lincoln gathered the men of his cabinet to read the Emancipation Proclamation to them, he said, "I do not wish your advice about this main matter.
. . . I must do the best I can and bear the responsibility."

This copy of the Emancipation Proclamation was printed with two U.S. flags, an eagle, and a painting of Lincoln.

beginning on January 1, 1863. The **proclamation** did not actually free any slaves in the South, because the Confederacy did not accept the proclamation. However, many African Americans joined the Union army after the proclamation was given. The proclamation also made it clear that if the Union won the war, the slaves in the South would be free.

Louisiana's Native Guard Joins the Union

Louisiana had some laws that were different from those of other states. In Louisiana, African Americans who were free people and who owned land were allowed to form their own **militia** units. Other states did not allow this.

African Americans in Louisiana organized themselves into militia groups called the Louisiana Native Guard. When Major General Butler called on African Americans to join the Union army on August 22, 1862, men from the Native Guard, as well as former slaves from other places, signed on to serve.

This print shows members of the Native Guard in 1863, guarding a railroad site for the Union.

On September 27, 1862, members of the Native Guard became the first African American soldiers to be **sworn** into the Union army. The citizens of Louisiana were very angry that former slaves were armed and ready to fight for the Union.

The men in the Native Guard fought hard for the Union. They also guarded war prisoners, built forts, and helped the Union in other ways.

The Confederacy Suffers Without New Orleans

A Southern woman named Mary Chesnut kept a diary throughout the war. In it she wrote, "New Orleans gone—and with it the Confederacy. Are we not cut in two? That Mississippi [River] ruins us, if lost." With the fall of New Orleans, the Confederacy lost an important port. New Orleans could no longer receive goods from Europe and Mexico or ship goods abroad to bring in needed money. The Union could now send troops into the South from New Orleans. It also controlled the lower part of the Mississippi River, although, the Confederacy still controlled other parts of the river. Farragut continued to fight other battles on the river. By July 1863, the Union had taken control of the Mississippi River, an important gain for the Union.

GLOSSARY

admiral (AD-muh-rul) A naval officer of the highest rank.

blockade (blah-KAYD) Ships that block passage to ports to keep supplies from going in or out.

Civil War (SIH-vul WOR) The war fought between the Northern and Southern states of America from 1861 to 1865.

Confederates (kun-FEH-duh-rets) People who fought for the South during the Civil War.

Confederate States of America (kun-FEH-duh-ret STAYTS UV uh-MER-ih-kuh) A group of 11 Southern states that declared themselves separate from the United States in 1860–61.

Emancipation Proclamation (ih-man-sih-PAY-shun prah-kluh-MAY-shun) The document issued by Abraham Lincoln in 1862 that said slaves in rebelling states were free.

fleet (FLEET) Many ships under the command of one person.

foster (FOS-tur) Not related by birth.

governor (GUH-vuh-nur) An official elected as head of a U.S. state.

militia (muh-LIH-shuh) A group of people who are trained and ready to fight in an emergency.

proclamation (proh-kluh-MAY-shun) An official announcement.

slavery (SLAY-vuh-ree) The system of one person "owning" another.

surrender (suh-REN-dur) To give up.

sworn (SWORN) To have made a solemn promise.

Union (YOON-yun) The Northern states during the Civil War.

War of 1812 (WOR UV AY-teen TWELV) A war between the United States and Great Britain, fought from 1812 to 1815.

West Indies (WEST IN-deez) The chain of islands lying between the United States and South America.

INDEX

PRIMARY SOURCES

Page 5: Photograph of Abraham Lincoln. By Alexander Gardner (1863). From the Library of Congress. **Page 6**: Lithograph of battle between the *Monitor* and the *Merrimack*, fought on March 9, 1862 (1889). From Hulton Archive. **Page 9**: Lithograph of blockade of the Mississippi River by Admiral Porter's fleet. By Currier and Ives (1863). From the Library of Congress. **Page 11**: Engraving of Admiral David.G. Farragut. By Geo. E. Perine. From the New York Public Library. **Page 12**: Print *Battles and Leaders of the Civil War* shows Farragut's fleet bombarding Fort Jackson and Fort St. Philip (1884–1887). From North Wind Picture Archives. **Page 14 (inset)**: Photograph of Admiral David.G. Farragut (1860–1865). From the National Archives and Records Administration. **Page 15**: Print showing General Johnson K. Duncan surrendering Forts Jackson and St. Philip to Commander David Porter. From North Wind Picture Archives. **Page 16**: Photograph of Major General Benjamin F. Butler (1860–1865). From the Library of Congress. **Page 17**: Wood engraving of starving people of New Orleans being fed by Union soldiers (1862). From the Library of Congress. **Page 19 (top)**: Lithograph of *Abraham Lincoln and his Emancipation Proclamation*. (1888). By Strobridge Lithograph Company. From the Library of Congress. **Page 19 (bottom)**: Engraving of Abraham Lincoln reading the Emancipation Proclamation to members of his Cabinet, July 22, 1862. By F.B. Carpenter. From the Library of Congress. **Page 21**: Engraving of Louisiana's "Native Guard" guarding the New Orleans, Opelousas, and Great Western Railroad. (1863). *Frank Leslie's Illustrated Newspaper*, March 7, 1863. From the Library of Congress.

WEB SITES

Due to the changing nature of internet links, PowerKids Press has developed an online list of Web sites related to the subject of this book. This site is updated regularly. Please use this link to access the list.

www.powerkidslinks.com/hfh/captno